CONOR McPHERSON

Born in Dublin in 1971, Conor McPherson attended University College Dublin, where he began to write and direct. He co-founded the Fly by Night Theatre Company, which performed new plays in Dublin's fringe venues.

Published plays include *Rum and Vodka, The Good Thief*, which won a Stewart Parker Award, *This Lime Tree Bower*, which won a Thames TV Award, a Guinness/National Theatre Ingenuity Award and the Meyer-Whitworth Award, *St Nicholas, The Weir* and *Dublin Carol. The Weir* won him the Most Promising Playwright Award from both the Evening Standard and the Critics' Circle and went on to win the Laurence Olivier Award for Best Play. It ran for eighteen months in the West End of London and played successfully on Broadway. *Dublin Carol* has been nominated for both Best Production at the Dublin Theatre Festival 2000 and Best Play, Irish Times/ESB Awards for 2000.

His script for *I Went Down* won Best Screenplay at the San Sebastian Film Festival. *Saltwater*, which he wrote and directed, won numerous European awards, including the CICAE Award for Best Film at Berlin.

In the same series

PORT AUTHORITY

NICK HERN BOOKS
London
www.nickhernbooks.co.uk

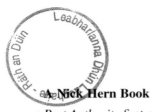

A Nick Hern Book

Port Authority first published in Great Britain in 2001
as a paperback original by Nick Hern Books Limited,
14 Larden Road, London W3 7ST

Front cover: Simon Williams Design

Typeset by Country Setting, Kingsdown, Kent CT14 8ES
Printed in Great Britain by Biddles, Guildford

ISBN 1 85459 625 X

Port Authority was first produced by the Gate Theatre, Dublin, at the New Ambassadors Theatre, London, in association with Ambassador Theatre Group and Old Vic Productions on 22 February 2001. The play opened at the Gate Theatre, Dublin, on 24 April 2001. The cast, in order of appearance, was:

KEVIN   Éanna MacLiam
DERMOT   Stephen Brennan
JOE   Jim Norton

Directed by Conor McPherson
Set design and costumes by Eileen Diss
Lighting Designer Mick Hughes

Author's Note

The play is set in the theatre.

PORT AUTHORITY

Characters

KEVIN, *maybe twenty*
DERMOT, *late thirties? mid thirties?*
JOE, *seventy-odd*

1
KEVIN

I moved out in the summer.
The house was in Donnycarney and four of us were
going to share it.
My folks were not happy about it.
The mad thing was I could see their point.
It was kind of stupid.
I had no job and I didn't know what I wanted to do.
Moving out was like pretending to make a decision.
My dad gave me a lift down to Donnycarney.
With all my clothes in black bin-liners.
It was a bright Sunday afternoon.
I nearly said, 'I'll see you later.'
But this was supposed to be for good.
What a joke.
I was moving in with Davy Rose and a guy called Speedy.
I was mates with Davy.
To everybody else in Dublin he was Mad Davy Rose, hammered
on Scrumpy Jack.
But I saw the normal side to him and he spoke to me
about stuff and, you know?
Speedy was more Davy's friend than mine.
Although I could hardly see how anyone could be friends
with Speedy at all.
He always seemed to me to be unbelievably stupid.
He definitely had a learning disorder or something.
Mostly he was just out of it, but even sober I couldn't
make head nor tail of him.
It was like he was excited by being bored.
I had nothing in common with him.
He was asleep in the back garden when I went through.
Davy was sitting in an old deckchair, drinking cider
and playing Billy Idol on his ghettoblaster.
He was in a state of agitation because he was in the

process of being dumped by this girl with blue hair
from Beaumount.
He was all distracted, talking about hopping on his
bike going up to annoy her.
I didn't want him to leave me on my own with Speedy
so I made him come down to the off-licence with me
and I got us more Scrumpy.
And we just went back and kept drinking.
Davy was searching through Speedy's pockets for smokes
and I was casually inquiring where Clare was.
She was moving in as well.
Everybody in Dublin was in love with her.
She was buds with me and Davy but she tended to go out
with headbangers. Or lads who thought they were, anyway.
She was always with some spiky-haired crusty who you
could see was from Dublin 4 or somewhere, putting on
a bit of an accent.
They were all rich and spoiled and better looking than
any of us.
Davy said he hadn't seen her.
So we got fairly pissed there in the garden and then I
went up to see which room was mine.
I had the bedroom at the back.
Davy had the attic conversion.
Clare had the bedroom at the front.
Speedy was in the boxroom.
We were all paying thirty quid, except Speedy who was paying
   twenty.
All was in my room was a bed and a chair.
I was in my sleeping bag all night lying there
awake listening to hear if I could Clare come in
but all I could hear were all the sounds that made me
try to imagine I was still at home.
But it didn't work.
In the morning I borrowed Davy's bike and I went down
to Kilbarrack to sign on and sort out rent allowance.
And when I got back it was just Speedy sitting there
watching Richard and Judy.
He nodded at me and I sat down there near him.
But he was genuinely watching Richard and Judy.

I was nearly afraid to say anything in case he missed
something.

He was eating rice krispies like he was on his way out
to work in a minute or something.

As if, you know.

And he suddenly starts saying, still not looking at me,
about how last Friday a guy from a band from Donaghmede
had called down with this small goth girl who was a
notorious slut.

And your man was in the back room with Davy jamming
on these two bases that were in there.

And your one asks Speedy if his has any hash and he
had so they went up to the boxroom and had a spliff
and all of a sudden they got stuck into each other,
having a sneaky ride.

And Speedy was trying to listen out to hear if he could
still hear your man jamming with Davy and he wasn't
coming up. But your one was starting to make so much
noise that Speedy just got too nervous so he just went
into the jacks and pulled himself off.

And he said all this to me just like that.

And I was just sitting there staring at the side of
his head, thinking that there was nothing he could
ever say that could interest me beyond the terrible
notion that I cared absolutely nothing for this fellow
human being. And that if he died I'd feel nothing.

And we sat there in this room for a while until I
could barely stand it.

Until I casually asked him if he knew when Clare was
moving in.

But there was nothing about Speedy to suggest that anyone
had just spoken to him.

And I was trying to decide whether to ask him again or
just fuck off out or something and he just goes, 'She's
here.'

2
DERMOT

Dinner. Friday night. O'Hagan's house.
A kind of a welcome to the fold.
And the elation of a huge salary in an interesting
job and having impressed these clean-shaven tailor-made
suits was clashing with the embarrassment of having
to present Mary to them.
Suddenly I was thinking about my wife.
It was alright when I was at Whelan's.
All the wives looked the same.
Down at the Christmas do in the Old Sheiling.
We moaned about them at the bar.
The way they were squealing at each other.
Hysterical, at being out of the house.
Just a few weeks before I'd been looking for some
old accountancy textbooks in the press in the bedroom
and a load of chocolate fell out on top of me.
And I just didn't even bother, you know that way?
She took up half the couch and watched Eastenders.
And I sat in the boxroom brushing up for the interview.
O'Hagan had rang me himself personally to tell me I'd
got it.
Cocktails in Gogarty's Monday night to say hello.
Griffen, Staunton, Crawford. Strong handshakes.
What I presumed was Armani. All ex-rugby.
And then one or two of their wives suddenly.
And I was like, 'Holy fuck, easy Tiger!'
Me in my Penny's blazer and my loafers from Dunnes.
Hardly able, but trying to swallow these Glenmorangies
being pressed into my fist.
Swaying in the door.
Mary and Colm curled up in the living room watching
Friends.
Colm. Nine years of age. Constant cold.

Useless at sports.

Bullied until third class.

Until Mary went down and spoke to the head.

Went down on her own.

Because there was simply only so much I could fit in.

And the head dealt with it.

And I drove Mary and Colm wherever they wanted to go
at the weekends, and although I wouldn't say I was
necessarily a quiet person, I hardly said a fucking
word.

Dinner in O'Hagan's house. Friday night.

I whined at Mary about how I needed to dress better.
She took me from shop to shop and I shelled out for
three suits. Cotton shirts. Silk ties.

Catching Mary smiling and seeing what there was to see
in her when we were younger, but we weren't younger now
and I told her that dinner at O'Hagan's was staff only.

No wives. That was another night.

And for once I had something to treasure, that I was
looking forward to.

A glittering jewel on the mountain at the top
of Friday.

And me trudging towards it not wanting to get there too
quickly.

Enjoying it in the middle distance.

Because I could see it and it was mine.

And it was going to happen.

3
JOE

Sister Pat knocked while I was getting dressed.
I could smell breakfast being served.
It was the first morning I'd felt hungry in ages.
She had a little box wrapped in brown paper.
It was addressed to me, but at my son's house.
His wife, Lisa, had dropped it in to me on her way to work.
Sister Pat was the closest thing I had to a friend, really.
She was the same age as a lot of the residents
but like that old expression, young at heart.
As opposed to me who was just bloody immature.
'It's not your birthday or something, is it?'
She says.
'No, my birthday's not 'til June.' I go.
My birthday's not 'til June! Like it'd make a difference!
Sure I hadn't had a birthday present in years, sure!
Who'd be sending an old curmudgeon birthday presents?
And not on his birthday.
I'm not that popular.
Well. I felt like a bit of a twit standing there
holding it.
It was very light. But there was definitely something in it.
For a religious, Sister Pat had a lot of little girl
in her.
She was being nosey, standing there waiting for me
to open it. But, like the bold child she knew she was,
she knew I was too awkward to tell her to clear off
the hell there out of it.
'Are you not going to open it?' She goes.
'I am.' I say.
Little box covered in brown paper.
Dun Laoghaire postmark.
'I'm going to wait 'til I have my breakfast,' I say.
'And I'll open it when I'm drinking my tea.'

'Do you know what you are?' she says to me,
'You're very vain.'
And she left then.
I knew what she meant, but she said things like that
and there was no real anger in it.
And it didn't really make me feel anything really either.
That's just what she was like.
Very direct.
A brilliant nun really.
A perfect bloody nun.
So I put on my jacket and took my stick and I went down
the corridor to the dining room.
There was about twenty of us in the home at that point.
Quick look around.
All present and correct.
No-one gone up to Beaumont in the middle of the night.
A few of us had sticks.
And a few were in wheelchairs.
But we were fairly agile now, not too bad.
I sat down there beside Jackie Fennel and Mary Larkin.
Who I mostly sat with when I ate.
Often me and Jackie'd wander round to the
bookies and get a bottle of stout in Tighe's.
And we'd put little bets on for Mary Larkin as well.
Local women worked in the home and they made you
your breakfast and they brought it over to you
and everything.
They were great to us.
So there we were and we spoke about the weather and
Mary Larkin's son, Peter, who was a guard and whose wife
was expecting another baby.
And Jackie Fennel was looking at the racing in the
Independent.
And now and again I'd think about the little box in
my pocket. And my arm'd move a little bit.
And after breakfast when everyone began to mooch
off for a chat or do their own thing, I sat there by
myself having a cup of tea while the local women
cleared up.
And I took out the box and I pulled at the string

which I put in my pocket.
And I pulled the paper off neatly because it was
all done neatly and I figured out how to get into
the cardboard.
And there was a little handwritten note and something
flat wrapped in tissue paper.
I pulled it out and I took away the tissue.
It was a small photo that I recognised.
And I knew what had happened and I didn't need to read
the note.

4
KEVIN

Clare was sticking luminous stars up on the wall
and ceiling of her room.
She wanted to paint the walls.
I said I didn't think we'd be let.
She said this was like a room where you sent your
granny to die.
Clare was very much sort of up to the minute.
When you saw her it took you a second but you
knew she was special.
She cared about her appearance but in a very discreet way.
She wore make-up but you couldn't see it.
She was definitely sexy but at the same time she was
one of the gang and very easy to be with.
For me anyway. And she saw me as like her mate.
Only when you saw her with a lot of other girls was
she like . . . a girl.
I was never one of those guys who hung around with
a lot of girls, as my friends.
If I knew a girl she was either the girlfriend of
someone I knew, or it was someone I was going out with.
So me and Clare was a weird thing for me.
So I was usually thinking about it a lot.
And wondering if . . . you know.
I was putting a plug on her CD player for her and I
was looking through her CDs.
She told me to take a tape out of a box beside her
bed. It was a demo tape. The guy she was seeing was
in a band.
Who wasn't? Everybody I knew was in half-assed bands.
Davy was in The Bangers.
He couldn't really play, but none of those bands
were any use.
I'd always have to go into their gigs in pubs in town.

There'd be six bands on, and then like a really drunk
band at the end that wasn't really a band, just
a mixture of blokes from the other bands and some eejits
who were just their mates.
And they'd get up and try and play something by Fugazi
or someone, but because it was really hard and no-one
could really play, they'd have to belt something easy
out like Anarchy in the UK.
These were pretty shite gigs now, you know? But I
went because all my mates were in that scene and you
could have a few beers and a bit of a laugh.
Everybody was a sort of a punk.
This was years after real punk.
But it was like a sub-grouping of people who weren't
into Bryan Adams or boy bands and all that.
I wasn't really a punk or anything.
I was just like one of their mates.
Guys like Davy who were notorious as mad bastards
all over Dublin. But who I saw the normal side of
because we'd grown up together and gone to school
together and all that.
Clare's boyfriend's tape was in a case
with a photocopied cover in it.
I stuck it in the machine and I was slightly pissed
off because they actually sounded quite good.
They sounded like REM or someone.
'They're really good, aren't they?' Clare goes.
And I had to say yeah, they were.
They'd played support to some quite big bands like
The Lemonheads and The Jesus and Mary Chain.
'We should get The Bangers to play with them sometime,'
I said.
Clare said yeah. But wasn't like a real yeah, more
like . . . yeah! Bit too enthusiastic.
The Bangers were playing that night and we were going
in to see them so I went into my room while Clare
got ready.
I hadn't unpacked any of my gear. I was pulling all my
clothes out but there was nowhere to put them, only
on the chair. So I put some trousers on the seat and

and some tops on the back, and my trainers underneath.
And I stood back surveying this.
Thinking I had to get much more organised.
But who was I fooling. I was already useless.
Like I was starving and I'd no idea even if there was
any food in the house.
I heard the shower go on and I could hear Clare going
'Oh my God!' at the state of the bathroom.
And later on we were down at the bus stop on the
Malahide Road.
It was a gorgeous summer's evening.
All amber and a cool breeze.
Clare had one of her runners off shaking a little
stone out of it.
I was leaning there looking at the mountains.
And Clare said up to me, she was kneeling on the ground,
'Are you alright ?'
And I was looking at the mountains and nodding.
But I didn't think she could see me, so I said,
'Yeah, I'm fine.'

5
DERMOT

Den duh duh.
I was standing on the Dart.
There were plenty of seats but I don't know.
I couldn't sit.
I didn't need to.
All the kids in the latest gear.
Me. Okay older. Okay a bit pudgy.
But none of them had an idea where I was headed.
The windows were black, only a burst of orange in the
stations or distant street lamps.
I was watching out for Sutton Cross.
Right there. On my own.
Holding on to a thing. A pole.
And people were getting on, getting off, whatever.
Not too busy because this was the opposite direction
to town. But I was nicely oblivious because I was sort
of plunging or something.
Banging right there into the peninsula from Raheny.
I kept looking up at the map. Like I didn't know.
Mary'd dropped me down to Raheny on her way to a hen
night. And I walked straight over to the station
until I saw her brakelights turn down at the village.
And I was back across over at the boozer like a shot.
Taking my time. Few little G&T's.
Few little ones in the afternoon as well.
At home while Mary was at the shops.
Before my shower.
Nice form. All the young loolas coming into the pub.
To spend the night here and wobble home, rowing with
the girlfriend.
They could have it.
Three G&T's later I was down on the platform.
Nicely.

Standing there on the train. Up through Howth Junction.
Bayside.

Bang Bang.

Nearly missed fucking Sutton.

Off I hopped. Straight over to the Marine Hotel, no
messing.

Had O'Hagan's address, but I needed a few directions.
Few G&T's later I felt fully equipped.

You can't ever go off half-cocked, half-medicated into
unchartered waters, you'll be eaten alive.

O'Hagan's were one of, if not the most successful
money managers in the country. They had all the big
musicians and broadcasters and all the big writers and
everyone. O'Hagan was a celebrity in his own right.
All the big fashion designers and all.

Christ knew who'd be up at this thing.

So I hung on to his gate for a few minutes snorting
up any snot I wanted to get rid of,

the sea stretching off towards the lights of the
Southside.

And I was veering up his driveway, up to these
steps going up to his door, thinking maybe I'd
overdone it on the G&T's, 'cause there'd be plenty
of booze inside, and I had this great revelation -
that it was too fucking late to do anything about it now!
I didn't even care anymore. So when I found the bell I
gave it a right couple of rings to signal my confident
arrival.

I was imagining church bells ringing out all across
the country. And a little blondie yoke with no straps
on her dress and her tits held up with wire opens the
door and says, 'Hello!'

'Hello!' I say, lobbing a leg over the threshold
and yanking at the sleeve of my anorak.

'Everybody's here,' she says.

'They are now!' says I.

And she doesn't really hear me and she carries my coat
off into the house.

And it reminded me of when I was younger and my mum
tried to get me into a posh school in Dublin run by

the Jesuits. It was all wooden staircases and arched
hallways. Did I get in?
Did I fuck!
She hadn't a notion, my mother.
And that's what this house was like.
Only all white. White on the walls and white funny
carpet like a tight fishing net.
White little seats everywhere.
And a weird buzzing noise which I realised was people
talking to each other.
And the blondie girl gives me champagne no less
and brings me into the drawing room while I'm
looking at her back.
But I don't know a sinner so I whore away at my glass
and there's a tray with more and I take two.
And then 'Dermot!' It's fucking O'Hagan's wife.
Which is okay in itself.
But that she's basically wearing what looks to me like
a piece of pink tissue paper and her tits are basically
hanging out is giving me a problem.
And it's all see-through, but her tits are basically
outside it and she's going 'How are you feeling?'
And I'm like 'Yeah, yeah . . . ' Like I'm cool.
but the controllers in your head who are telling
you that you have to live with your future self
are filing this moment away under Moronic Moments
To Relive Again And Again.
And for some reason I'm thinking about when I was 19
and I used to cycle around on my sister's bike, and
my clothes were old. Not old like you Saying Who You
Were. But old like you'd had them a few years and the
fibres were old in them. And they were all a bit grey
and even though you didn't, you probably felt like
you were probably into little girls. That you felt like
you looked like you liked little girls.
And these thoughts were obviously evident in my face
so O'Hagan's wife is saying 'Don't be intimidated!'
And she takes my arm and starts saying 'Come on, we're
all going to eat now.' And she's pulling me along and
I feel like I'm going to go over on my snot so I'm

walking all funny.

And then all of a sud we're going down a spiral staircase.
And then we're at the bottom and I'm like 'How the
fuck did I manage that?' And sort of congratulating myself
and I hear all this 'Dermot!' 'Dermot!' 'Over here!'
And there they all are. O'Hagan, Crawford, Staunton,
all sitting down to eat rabbits while a woman like my
mum is putting roast 'dates* down in a big flat bowl.
And Crawford is saying something like 'Dermot, don't
ever be afraid of roast potatoes,' or something.
And I go, 'What the fuck are you saying?'
But nobody hears me.
And I feel a row coming on, but I'm on top of it.
And I think that I'll probably just break something later instead.
And the little blondie one seems to be in charge of everything.
But like she's been hired, at the same time she's like
everyone's friend. And they all call her Charlotte and
so do I because she's pumping the wine into everybody
and constantly opening bottles.
And I realise that all the women at the table are
like what I see in Mary's magazines.
All dressed like they always are, just before it all
has to come off. Because it just has to.
And I'm watching Charlotte's severe fringe and the
freckles across her nose and her tan and O'Hagan's wife
plonks down right opposite me.
And I try to distract myself by working out if we're
on benches or seats, but if I check I'm a goner.
So I just silently place my hands on the table.
My head is the moon and I've got to keep it away from
the earth.
I use my arms to do this.
And I use O'Hagan's wife's mostly visible tits to
keep the astronauts from panicking.
We panic and we're gone.
So we're using O'Hagan's wife's tits as a vital NASA
supply to balance our brains. Because we can, in our
distraction, act automatically, and just use our

*(potatoes)

reflexes, which are nature's cause and effect certainties.
And slowly I notice that everything has gone very
quiet.
And I hear someone say 'Dermot?'
And I realise that someone must have just asked me
a question.
And everyone's just twigged why the fuck I can't answer.
And O'Hagan's wife has a big reddener and she's
got her napkin practically up at her neck.
And I have this overwhelming urge to use the toilet.
And not just use the toilet.
Use the fact that it has walls.
And that no-one has X-ray eyes.
But of course they do, don't they?
Of course they fucking do.

6
JOE

I'm going to tell you something, right?
I was always just like everybody else.
Do you get me?
There was simply never any question about it.
You saw me with a bunch of people, you wouldn't
notice me.
I never thought about myself.
I saw the world as a very organised place that was
easy to negotiate. I saw people as generally good
and if there were blackguards around the place -
well that's what they were. Blackguards.
I met my wife, Liz, when I was working up in
Cadbury's.
I was older than her and I'd sort of risen up through
the ranks a bit by then and she was working on the floor.
Which made it a bit difficult to bump into her.
But I always had my eye on her. Don't know why.
She had thick little legs. She was small and a bit
                    . . . busty I suppose.
Got my chance to ask her up at the Christmas dance 1956.
To my astonishment she had no boyfriend and we started
going out together.
I had a pretty flash car, an Austin, and I was still
living with the parentals, so I had a few bob.
And Liz was basically a smasher in many ways.
Always laughing. Always in good form.
If there was an awkward silence, she just hummed to
herself. Do you get me?
She was like me.
There was nothing neither wrong nor right about us.
I could easily stand in her parents living room at
Christmas time and she could easily sit in mine.
We got married in Cabra in 1960 and moved into a house

in Donnycarney.

In those days in Ireland like, you didn't have a lot
of the issues that you do now.

She cooked the dinner and packed in the job and I
earned the spons. That was it. There was none of your
everyone's on valium because they're all confused about
who they are.

Listen, I'm not saying that things were better then
than now, only different and you didn't need to be asking
all the questions you do now. And to tell you the truth
that suited me. That suited me down to the
ground. Because when the time came for me to have
to start asking questions, let me tell you at the time,
I could've done without it.

Or maybe I'm glad it happened.

You see? I've no idea about myself!

I don't even know if I'm happy or sad!

But how and ever. Liz became pregnant with Stephen
in '61. And two years later we had Tania.

Not a family name. Liz saw it in a film.

Oh, the times they were a changing, for sure.

And after a few years and the kids were that bit older
and I was still earning a nice few bob, we decided
to move to a bigger house.

A beautiful house up in Sutton.

Right there on the peninsula.

7
KEVIN

It was an absolutely dismal night for The Bangers.
It was the first time they'd headlined their own gig.
So they were paying for the rent on the venue
and they'd had to hire the P.A.
There were supposed to be three bands, one of who,
the Lepers had a big following on their own.
But they'd had to cancel because one of them had lost
a finger in the sheet metal factory where he worked.
Yeah, yeah, the jokes about the leper who'd lost his
finger were endless.
A completely brutal band from Skerries were on.
It was ten o'clock and there were only about fifteen
people in the place.
Davy was just getting hammered on Scrumpy Jack.
He had a bag of cans under the table.
He was talking about not going on.
Scampi, The Bangers' lead singer was saying they might
as well now they were here. Their guitar player
Vinnie Harper said he couldn't give a shit either way.
Danny the drummer had shifted this small goth chick
so he wasn't going anywhere.
It was lashing rain outside and the whole thing was
just generally a bit depressing.
I was embarrassed for them as well because Clare
had managed to drag her boyfriend along.
Not only was he a proper musician and actually worked,
he had a job in a printers, he was actually a nice guy.
His name was Declan. Into that whole suede jacket,
jeans and boots vibe.
Big sideburns on him.
And because Clare usually went out with terrible fucking
morons I reckoned this might be the real thing.
She wasn't all over him or anything.

You could just tell she was into him.
Whenever he said anything, well you had to shout really
at those gigs, she was right in there. Leaning in.
Giving him her ear. Nodding. Following him. Getting it,
you know?
I was beginning to feel sick of the whole not-living-with-
your-folks thing.
Clare couldn't stand Speedy. He was just constantly
out of it. He was filthy and he always ate all her food.
It was a bad atmosphere.
Davy's genius solution was to have a big housewarming.
party to clear the air.
Without asking any of us he'd printed up flyers and
fucking everyone in Dublin seemed to have one.
There was still two weeks to go and the word of mouth
was becoming enormous.
I was seriously thinking about moving back home
because basically it was going to be mental, the
neighbours would definitely be calling the guards
and the landlord who was a bit of a cunt anyway would
have us all out on our snot in a heartbeat.
So there I was on this disastrous night for
The Bangers and I was more or less lost in thought.
Davy had finally been persuaded to go on.
Vinnie Harper was only starting to tune up his guitar
but Scampi just shouts 'We're The Bangers!'
And Davy just sort of jumped into the drumkit and
they were away.
A couple of drunk crusties started moshing around
a bit, but the truth was I'd never heard them sound worse.
Clare's boyfriend sat there with a stunned look of morbid
interest. And me and Clare just looked at each other
and burst out laughing. And I just went (mimes lifting
glass to his mouth) And she goes (Thumbs up sign)
So I wandered off downstairs to the empty bar.
Only little old men drank in here and it was dead.
I stood there staring up at an old photo of some
priests holding up a big cheque and someone slapped
me lightly across the face.
It was the girl working behind the counter.

She was my age and she had lots of curly hair.

'Wakey wakey', she goes.

I snapped out of it and asked her for two pints of
Bulmers

'You upstairs?' she asks me, sort of looking at me.

'Yeah,' I said. 'It's fucking awful.'

And later on I was sitting in Jimmy Dean's diner
with Clare and her boyfriend. And Davy was getting sick
in the jacks.

And the barmaid who'd slapped me, whose name was
Trish came in and joined us.

And I wasn't completely surprised.

Because when I'd asked her to she said she definitely
might alright.

8
DERMOT

Don't ever try to work anything out.
Because you don't know - and you never will.
And even if you do, it'll be too late to do anything
about it anyway.
Just don't bother. You'd think I'd been a disaster
at O'Hagan's party?
A danger to shipping?
An embarrassment at the very least, ha?
A tableful of people had just watched me transfixed,
I mean transported by my bosses wife's boobs.
A tableful of whatdoyoucallit, your colleagues.
But nothing was normal about this.
Are you normal?
'Cause if you think you are - you'll be like me.
Sitting on the toilet.
Clenching my fists and unclenching them.
Rocking back and forth.
Staring into the fact that I'd blown it.
Blown it all to hell up the wazoo.
Trying to ignore the little knocks at the door.
No-one was going to throw me out. I'd leave
of my own accord when I was good and ready, clutching
the last shreds of my dignity on my own thank you
very much.
But it was the way O'Hagan's wife said my name.
'Dermot?' she said. 'Are you alright?'
The way whe said it.
Through the door.
There was no punishment in it.
No judgement or something.
Unbelievably.
It made me open the door.
So I stood there and I started to say how sorry I

was and too much to drink and so on.

But she just laughed a little sad laugh.

And placed a reassuring hand on my arm.

And I heard O'Hagan and the others shouting from the kitchen.

'Dermo!' O'Hagan was going. 'Get yourself back in here and have your sweet, you fucking eejit!'

And I went back in there with his wife.

What is it? Money? Or Royalty or something?

Where the rules are different.

But I should have twigged that something was weird about all this ages before.

Right there in the beginning.

At the interview.

I mean, I don't think they even asked me about three questions. Three maybe. And they were like general what do you make of the present state of affairs as they stand at the moment type questions. Rhetorical, even, like, 'Who can say what way the bloody country is going, ha?'

I mean, how do you answer?

You know?

You sort of go, 'Well, it's very hard to say, isn't it?' That's all I could do.

And O'Hagan just goes, 'Well everything we've heard about you is very impressive, and we'll be in touch.'

Heard what about me?

That I'd never actually passed my ACCA?

Or that in the eighteen months I'd worked in Denis Mahony's I never sold a single car? Not one!

Or what, that I'd been sacked out of Whelan's for so-called sexual harrassment? Of, supposedly, another man!

What? That I was just generally a bit of a disaster?

Whatever they'd heard, I wasn't going to question it!

They'd given me the job and here I was.

I mean I sat back down there at the table and I was *totally* accepted.

And I hadn't even started working yet, you know?

Well, what the fuck.

Here were coming the cigars and I took one and
someone else's wife lit it for me.
And O'Hagan comes down beside me.
His big arm around my shoulders.
'You're a man after my own heart,' he goes, 'Ha? Ha?'
Me smiling and nodding, pretending I know what the fuck
is going on.
And then he goes 'You ever heard of The Bangers?'
Had I what?
They were the biggest thing out of Ireland since The
Cranberries. They were going to be as big as U2.
Huge in the States.
'We look after them,' he says, 'They're kicking off
their tour in Los Angeles St. Patrick's weekend. We're
all going to go. Are you free?' He says to me.
Well it was that or round to Mary's mother's house for
corned beef and cabbage and rock hard potatoes.
So I thought about it.
For about a millisecond.
The big blank head on me.

9
JOE

You want a tip?
When you dream in the night, just wake up, forget
about it, get on with it, get up in the morning and
have your breakfast and go to work.
Be courteous in your job and use your manners.
'Cause if you dream that someone's loving you and you
wake up looking for them and sending signals to all
and sundry around you in the daytime, saying was it
you? Was it you who loved me?
You'll fucking find them, mark my words.
They'll come to you.
They'll seem different.
Like someone who's changed over the years like you
knew them as a child. But it'll be them.
And all that longing that's in you.
When you thought you'd never meet again and a dam
bursts.
It's all in you.
And for an ordinary man like me to discover that.
Well it was slightly the end of the world there for a
little while.
What happened was this.
When we moved up to the peninsula, up to Sutton, our
nextdoor neighbours invited us into a party in their
house one Saturday night.
His name was Tommy Ross and his wife's name was Marion.
They were having a family do.
It was Tommy's parents' anniversary and they were throwing
a bit of a bash.
I'd only ever chatted to him a little bit maybe in the
garden in the morning. I'd never spoken to her.
Liz, my wife, had tended to stay friendly with her
old pals from Cadbury's and from where we'd lived in

Donnycarney.

Stephen was ten and Tania was eight.

Naturally, they fought like tigers, so even though
we were only going next door for a few hours Liz's
sister, Aunty Carmel, came up to babysit and we were
able to go.

And even though we didn't know anyone at all, you see
in those days you just spoke to people.

Even though then it was like it is now and people
had a few bob.

We'd bought a table set for Tom's parents and we
chatted to them for a while.

And I spoke to one of Tom's brothers, Frank and
his wife, Phyllis and Liz was chatting to another
sister, Bernie.

And it was all very pleasant.

In those days I drank bottles of Smithwicks.

And there was all sixpacks of Smithwicks and Guinness
and Harp all stacked up in the garage, and all the
nieces and nephews'd bring some in and take out the
empties and all this and it was about ten o'clock and
very pleasant.

The first one or two early risers might have started
to leave, but things were more or less in full swing.

And I went into the kitchen at one point to get myself
another ham sandwich or an egg sandwich and I got
talking to Tom Ross's wife, Marion, and as we'd never
really spoken before, it was only natural that we
should fill in a lot of history, being new neighbours.

Now before you start thinking, 'Yo ho! Here's where it
gets good!' let me explain that there were other
people in the kitchen and this was all normal and
acceptable.

Only, the night before I'd had a dream that I was down
at this river and there was a woman there with jet
black hair and the unconditional no-nonsense acceptance
I'd felt was like, when I woke up, that I'd lost a part
of myself.

Not that Marion looked anything like this woman in the
dream.

She looked nothing like her.
She had short fair hair and a little pug nose.
And she was telling me about the people who'd lived
next door before we moved in and how horrible
they were, and I was just staring at her for some reason
and the strange way she twisted her jaw when she
became full of good humoured bad thoughts about
people she was criticising.
And I was desperately trying to cop onto myself.
And eat this bloody ham sandwich, but there was no
water in my mouth so I was drinking too much Smithwicks.
But it all seemed so bloody unimportant when I
watched her little leg spin whenever she heard a song
she liked come on.
So I made sure we made our way out to the living room
and I stood there with my arm on Liz for the rest
of the night.
With everyone, including Marion, oblivious of what had
just happened to me.
And me putting it all out of my mind hopelessly
as a passing nonsense that'd do nobody any good in
the long run.
And you fool yourself that God hasn't seen you.
But there were a few little involuntary twitches in
my legs and hands for the next hour or two until we
went to bed, let me tell you!
                              . . . I put it down to the drink.
And of course to that bloody dream I'd had.
And that was the end of that.
But, of course it was impossible for him not to,
God had seen me.

10
KEVIN

I had a comfortable time then.
Trish was a student at NCAD.
And she worked in the pub in the evenings.
I was like a little old man there.
Going in. Sitting up there watching the snooker.
Having a pint or two.
She lived around the corner in a flat on Parliament
Street.
We fucked all night all the time.
She'd shake her head, all her curly hair hitting me
in the face.
All her pent-up frustrations about being from the
country.
Her legs around mine so I couldn't get away.
The condom coming off and bursting and every fucking
thing.
She didn't speak to me much though.
Not about anything important.
You even looked at her too long, I mean admiringly,
she'd come straight over and punch you in the chest,
wanting to know what you were staring at.
But other things like, you'd be standing there in the
Spar buying a can of Coke and her hand would slip into
mine, absent-mindedly, and automatic, no strings
attached, just proper love.
The light blazing across her face when we were sitting
on the bus, upstairs at the front.
Going out through Fairview up to Donnycarney.
She loved Davy.
They were the same.
They wanted more than the world had to give them.
She drank and dragged me to my feet to dance, her
hand clamped on my arse.

Clare was confused by her a bit I think.
And, maybe it was because, all of a sud, here
was something me and Clare couldn't talk about.
All of us there hanging round the house.
Clare giving Davy a hard time about the whole
of Dublin being invited to the housewarming.
Davy in a stupor.
Speedy mostly asleep.
I was watching the Simpsons and I got up to make a
cup of coffee.
And Trish and Clare were standing there in the kitchen
talking and I moved between them like I wasn't welcome.
Like I needed a friend.
And we went down to the pub and Trish got up to get
a round and I was eating some crisps and I caught
Clare looking at me and we started laughing.
Well it was that or bursting into tears or some fucking thing.
Later on in the chipper Clare began to get organised
about we had to go to the supermarket the next day
because if Davy wasn't going to do anything about this
party, then we had to.
Trish was pretending her battered sausage was someone's
dick. She only had a grey vest top on.
And later on she gave me the most unbelievable blow job.
I nearly came all over the place.
You see someone laughing with your spunk all over them,
let's face it you're on to a good thing.
All in her curly hair and all.
And that night we fell asleep together for the first time.
She was late for college and everything.
I had my jeans on and I was eating cornflakes there
in my bare feet and Clare comes into the kitchen
twirling car keys on her finger.
She'd borrowed her mam's Fiesta.
And we drove down to Superquinn in Sutton Cross.
She had a silver bracelet on her left arm and she had
a tan and I was watching it when she changed gears.
And projecting ahead like we were married and this was
what we did all the time.
The little concentrated look on her face going up

through the traffic.
Her thin lips at all the bad drivers.
And I'd never done anything like this except with my
mum, pushing a trolley around the supermarket.
I just wanted to grab Clare right there.
She had sporty stripes down her pants.
She had no socks on.
And just, her stupid ankles there.
Like she'd never need to wear socks if she was with
me or something.
Obviously I was losing it, so I clamped my fingers
around the handle on the trolley.
And we both knew this housewarming thing was going
to be disastrous.
And I began to realise that Clare had to know there
was no point in buying stuff for a bunch of mentlers
who were going to come and just basically drink you
out of house and home.
And I knew that all this supermarket bullshit was because
Clare just wanted to spend some time with me again.
And she turned at one point and put her hand on my belly
while we were looking at frozen pizzas.
And for ages we couldn't move.

11
DERMOT

First class on a plane?
To America?
It's all napkins and tablecloths and 'You were drinking
the Chardonnay, Sir?'
It's stupid.
I don't know how much it costs, but we're
talking thousands, yeah?
And it was St. Patrick's weekend, so they were all there.
Adams, McGuinness, Reynolds, Cowan, Ahern, Eammon
Dunphy, Ian Dempsey, And me, and O'Hagan, and Crawford
Griffen, Staunton, and all their wives.
But no Mary.
She'd stood there in the shadow and the light there
on the landing, my hand on hers on the bannister.
'I have to go,' I said, 'They're making me.'
And fuck, she saw right through me.
She didn't say a fucking word.
But she'd clocked me.
I was snared.
But where do you go?
You stay where you are.
And she nodded and smiled and went off into the bathroom.
And I used the sound of the bath running to open the
drinks cabinet and help myself to some strange cocktail
which kicked in a little while later while I was
lying on the sofa thinking about LA.
And here I was!
On the broom broom.
And we're all getting up and walking around like
we're in a club or something.
Meeting and greeting. Pressing the flesh.
With the great and the good.
The air hostesses all licking up to us, everybody

laughing at everybody else's stupid comments.
But nothing could hide that there was a bit of
a smell of shit on the plane, like one of the
jacks was broken or something.
A smell to which I have to say I contributed
to with a couple of hefty pounds of crap myself.
It goes in, it comes out!
What are you going to do? Hold it in?
I stank up my bloody hotel room first thing as well.
We'd all been picked up by limos.
I was knackered and fairly drunk from the plane.
And The Banger's concert was that night.
'Don't go asleep, Dermot,' they were all warning me.
'The only way to beat the jet lag is to stay up.'
Stay up! I felt like it was half eleven at night
and I'd been in the pub all day.
Stay up . . .
I sat there on the bed in the hotel.
I had a load of rooms. One like a sitting room.
One for like having your nosh or to hold a
meeting in. And one like a proper hotel room with
a bed. Me in the middle. The stinky smell of my crap
all over the place.
Mary'd packed this pair of shorts she'd got me.
They were like cool combat shorts with big pockets
on the side of them.
So I put them on and went down looking for the bar.
But at reception they told me the bar didn't open until
like six or something ridiculous.
So I wandered back up to my room and I sat on the
balcony looking down into the empty pool, and I
made a right few dents into the minibar until the
phone finally rang and it was time to go down to the
lobby where we were all meeting our limo to take us
to see The Bangers.
But in truth we weren't going to see The Bangers.
We were going to The Banger's concert which is different.
We were going to be backstage in the VIP enclosure.
All O'Hagan and them and their wives all dressed casual,
all hip and laid back and not millionaires, all in their

brand new sparkling white nikes.
So if you said to me, 'What are The Bangers like live?'
I couldn't tell you.
But I can tell you that backstage is like something out
of Lord of the Rings.
You can see the stage and the speakers towering up and
all banners blowing in the wind like a castle and a little
village of people all milling around. All hoping that
some rubbish is going to be thrown out of the castle
one day, and by mistake there'll be something good
in it, like a diamond, and if you're the one that finds
it you're never going to have to work again or ever be
hungry anymore.
I was beginning to feel scared and the night air was
cold and I was trying to numb all my fears by drinking
vodka. And I got talking to some blonde girl and her
husband. He was English and on the off-chance that I
was someone important they were being very friendly
towards me. And they asked me if I wanted to take some
cocaine.
I'd never taken it in my life but I wanted anything to
take away these scary feelings I was having.
So we snorted this cocaine up our noses in a portaloo.
The smell of shit was overwhelming and a roar went up
from eighty thousand people and I spun out into the
night, quite convinced that bats were going to attack me.
And I had a bottle of vodka in my hand and I
cowered in the corner of a field, feeling that my life
was in great danger.
Until O'Hagan's wife found me and we went to some party
where I couldn't stay and the next thing I knew
I was back in the hotel room.
It had started to get bright.
I had my shorts on and I was looking at the weird
dimples on this girl's breast implants where it looked
all plastic.
And I was on the phone and I was talking to Mary.
She was down there in Artane at her parents' house on
the estate. She was on her mobile and nieces and nephews
were arriving for St. Patrick's Day.

I could hear them squealing.

She was standing there in the garden and I could imagine it.
All the sounds were all so innocent and somehow very
real. There was an echo which struck me as something
to do with the summer and I couldn't take it any more
so I said, 'Take it easy.' And I put the phone down.

And this girl on the bed was asleep and I was looking at
her vagina and wondering how old she was and who she
was, it was a plump dark line, and I was wondering if
this funny feeling of the carpet under my feet was
a feeling of remorse.

And I began to go asleep and the sun was beginning to
shriek in the windows.

And then later, O'Hagan was in the room and the girl
seemed to have gone.

And we were slowly playing with the minibar like it
was a minibar on the Titanic and we were divers from some
crazy museum.

And he told me that someone had made a terrible mistake.
Someone had recommended someone with the same name
as me to Crawford. Someone at his rugby club.

And they'd made the mistake of giving me the job.
Because they saw my CV first.
But I knew something like this was bound to happen.
He was apologising, saying it was a monumental cock-up.
And he'd only just found out.

But he eyed me steadily while he told me that if
I did anything stupid like trying to sue him, the
minute I met his lawyers I'd be dead in the water.
And I hadn't a chance.

I waved my hand limply.

We were both really out of it.

And he kept saying, Good man. Good man.

And I'd be reimbursed for my inconvenience.

It was just that they'd thought I was somebody else.

He stood at the wall.

And his wife kept ringing the room to see if he was
ready to go out for dinner.

And he told me his mother had died a few months ago
and she wanted, in her will, for some photo of herself

to be sent to some man who used to be their next door
neighbour.
He couldn't rest any more, he said, thinking about it.
'But I suppose,' he said, 'The past is over, isn't it?'
Later on they were all gone out to dinner and I was
on the phone, trying to find out how I could fly back
to Dublin.
But I can't remember too much of all this, understandably,
because it was all very much like some dream I was
having.
There's no way of saying it even without it all
seeming very strange to me.
But, like O'Hagan says, the past is over.
Isn't it?

12
JOE

In those days a lot of us could just about boil an
egg. Those of us who worked a lot.
There just wasn't the time.
There just wasn't the need.
Breakfast with the kids.
Soup and sandwiches at your lunch.
And off home to your shepherds pie or your few chops
for your tea. Sure you spent half your time trying to get it into
the kids, any way you could.
So when they found a cyst on one of Liz's ovaries
and the date was set for her to go in and have it done,
it was decided that Dermot and Tania would stay with
Liz's sister Aunty Carmel in Baldoyle.
We drove Liz up to the Bons on a Sunday.
We went into her little room and the kids sat on the
bed while she took her few bits out of her overnight
bag and got into her nightie.
And pretty soon the sister came in to say the
specialist was on his way.
So we all gave Liz a kiss and I drove the kids up to
Baldoyle.
Aunty Carmel gave us some mushroom omelettes and chips.
And when I left them there, there were no tears or no
messing.
This was an adventure for the kids there with their
cousins.
Sleeping in their cousins' beds and everything.
And I went home and ran a bath.
I'd barely seen Marion or Tommy Ross since their
party.
Which was probably a mistake in itself though.
Because, because I'd gotten a land for myself that
night in the kitchen with Marion, and if you don't

see the person and see all their little ways that make
them normal, you sort of, involuntarily romanticise
them, don't you?
It was like the next door neighbours' house was like
some kind of bizarre memorial or something.
To what, I don't know.
Some strange dream or the constant possibility that you
can get yourself a bit of a land for yourself, maybe.
And our house felt fierce empty in the morning.
And I phoned Aunty Carmel and spoke to the kids and
ate some bread and butter and tea.
And you know the way sometimes you go to work, but
everything's different and there's a calmness in you
that you didn't think it was possible for you to have?
A strange floaty day.
I suppose because your normal routine is that bit upset.
I left a little early and went up to the Bons where
Liz was fasting.
She was in good form and more looking forward to getting
it over with than afraid.
She was a real Dublin spirit.
And I spoke to the specialist, Mr. Ellis, and we were all
very businesslike all of a sudden, but it was time
to go and I dropped a load of chocolate off up to
Aunty Carmel's for the kids and the cousins.
But they were all out the back playing on a swing
they'd made from one of the trees, and they hardly
paid me any notice so I drove off home.
And there I was, sitting there watching the
news and thinking about maybe opening a tin of
beans or maybe nipping out for a fish and chip, when
perhaps you might say inevitably, the door bell rang,
and there was Marion with a plateful of dinner with
tinfoil over it.
Which, of course, as a Christian you have to appreciate
but because as well this person has reached mythic
proportions in your sense of what's right and wrong
and what can tip the balance into some kind of
unpredictable insanity you take the plate with slight
trepidation, don't you?

But of course she was completely innocent of anything
as, technically, we both were.

And she actually stood at the sink and did my breakfast
dishes while I ate this food that was very alien to
me and I didn't quite know what it was.

And she was inquiring after Liz and how we were all
coping.

And I was trying to work out if she'd done anything
to her appearance before dropping in.

Anything to make herself in any way more appealing
than she otherwise might've needed to.

And I was sitting there, deciding she hadn't, she was
wearing Scholl sandals and a scarf on her head.

And she suddenly stopped and said, 'Is that Bay Rum?'
which was something I usually used in my hair in those
days.

I said, yes, it was.

And she was slightly miles away like the smell or me
or both or whatever, reminded her of something.

And before she left she said she'd keep an eye on me
and if there was anything I needed done, washing
or anything, just to give her a shout.

And why I felt so bad without having done or said
anything bad, it was awful.

And I was afraid of my life that I'd be punished
somehow by Liz's operation going awry in some way
or that God was telling me he was taking her away because
I was really supposed to be with somebody else.

But, she was fine and clean as a whistle when I went in
to see her the next evening and Mr. Ellis was confident
she'd be home within the week.

Which I took as a sign that everything was alright
and normal in the world and not to be giving myself
heart attacks over nothing.

But it was a fine, bright April evening and Marion and
Tommy Ross called in to see how Liz was getting on and
did I want my dinner.

They had a little white dog with them on a leash and
they were going for a walk and asked me if I'd like
to join them but I felt so full of loss looking at

Marion pulling at the dog's leash that I had to say no.
And Tommy told me to call into them for a night cap
later and I said I would because I needed to get the
door shut so I could lean against the wall.
With like this image of Marion looking down at the
little dog and pulling at the leash, her elbow going up,
emblazoned into my eyes or something.
And I sat on the stairs and actually watched the house
get dark before I got up and went next door.
For a night cap.
Tommy brought me in and we chatted about various things,
like work and politics.
And Marion was upstairs with one of the kids who
Was getting a bit of a temperature.
But she soon came down and had a Bacardi and Coke
with us and I was about to push off, because I felt
I needed a few stiffeners at home to sort myself out.
And their little boy came down and he wasn't well
and Tommy brought him back up and Marion went to see
if she had the number of the doctor.
And for a minute I was alone there in their livingroom
and I was staring at a bookcase and I saw this black
and white picture of Marion when she was like only
a child. But she looked exactly the same.
And she was grinning into the camera with a look
halfway between innocence and a dawning mischief
that there were things in the world you could get
away with.
And I picked it up and I tried to put it in my pocket.
And Marion came back in and basically she caught me.
I pretended I was just wiping it on my jacket, like
it was a bit dusty or something.
And I was sort of going 'Is this you? Ha ha ha.'
But she had a cold serious look in her eyes and she just
said to me, 'Do you want that?'
And I was like, 'What? Are you mad? What do you mean?
Ha ha ha.'
But she was just 'Do you want that?'
And I didn't know what to say.
And she said, 'You can have it if you want it.'

She said, 'You can keep that. If you want it.'
And she was so calm about it in a way that I couldn't
understand that I nearly did. I nearly took it.
But of course all your dead relatives and teachers
from your youth and all the things that are basically
yourself are all there, aghast, and I just put it back
on the bookcase.
And I went towards the door which meant that I went
past her brown shoulder and out into the garden
and back into my house where I lay curled up on
the sofa, half expecting a soft knocking at the front
door or the window which never came.
And I knew that I couldn't take that photograph
because I was afraid to. And I was afraid to because
I didn't know why I wanted it.
And I felt like that was the truth.
And I barely ever saw or spoke to that woman again.
For better or for worse. Or both, mmm?
Because that's what you do.

13
KEVIN

Predictably by about one o'clock in the morning
panes of glass were broken in the living room door.
The guards had already been once to tell us to keep
the racket down.
An ambulance had been because some poor eejit had
gotten a hiding on his way to the party and he arrived
with his nose all over his face.
There was another fight brewing in the front garden
between the local hardchaws and a load of crusties
who hung out in town.
They were fucking beer cans at each other across the
street.
Speedy had fallen asleep in the toilet and the door was
locked. Davy finally had to kick it in so the girls
could have somewhere to have a slash.
The boys were all just doing it in the garden.
The smell of cider piss out the back was all over the
neighbourhood. It was like vinegar and the grass was
all dead.
There was just a mad atmosphere.
Davy opened up his plastic dustbin full of homebrew.
It was supposed to ferment for two months.
But he'd only started making it on Tuesday and everyone
was milling it.
Someone's dad was at the party, standing in the
hall, calm as you like, drinking a can of Royal Dutch
and talking to this really boring American guy who
always seemed to turn up everywhere.
A girl fell down the stairs and people were saying
we were going to have to call another ambulance.
And even though me and Clare had locked our bedroom
doors there were people in them, and it wasn't worth
the hassle trying to get them out.

We were all past caring.
I was standing in the back garden.
Someone had just handed me a goldfish in a little
plastic bag full of water.
Unbelievably it was still alive.
No-one knew where it came from.
There'd nearly been a mill when one of Clare's old
flames had tried to headbutt Declan, her new
boyfriend.
But it was over pretty quickly with Clare tearing
into your man, screaming insults into his face until
he just stood on his own over at the kitchen door,
hanging his head in an unbelievable wave of shame.
A little while before I'd seen Trish's curly hair under
the oil tank. She was snogging this guy in a big
woolly hat. And then she stood up and turned and
saw me and I totally believed her as she staggered
away saying, 'I thought that was you!', her
hands up to her face, starting to laugh.
The chap under the oil tank reached up to her and let
out an indistinguishable 'Ughhh . . . ' protesting to
her. And she just turned and gave him the most almighty
kick in the face I've ever seen. He was too drunk to
feel it and he was asleep immediately.
It was that type of atmosphere.
Scampi had pulled Davy's amp out into the garden and
he was trying to persuade the Bangers to crank up and
do a few songs.
And suddenly a football appeared and there was an
impromptu game in full swing with no teams and no
goalposts, just loads of random boots and people running
around with a mad sense of purpose.
I went over to the side of the house and stood in the
passage to protect the little fish.
I kicked some full cans of Scrumpy in the darkness and
I started to drink them.
Some girl tried to snog me for a minute but I was rapidly
becoming just generally incapable.
And someone ran up to me and said 'Paul McCartney's
actually here!'

And I suddenly felt like there was just nowhere to go.
And the police arrived again and soon it was all over.
Davy was nearly arrested only Clare intervened on his
behalf saying he was mentally ill.
And I just basically stayed up in the garden all night
wandering around drinking from various cans that were
scattered about.
And when it was bright I went up to my room to have
a sleep but there were people there already.
So I tapped on Clare's door and went in.
She lay on her side, her eyes were open.
Declan was asleep with his arm round her.
I sat down beside the bed with her looking at me.
And I gave her a look that said, 'Well, that's that.'
And she smiled and she slowly got up to put some
clothes on, her brown skin shining in the morning light.
And went downstairs, not saying anything and we
went for a walk.
We walked down the Malahide Road, down to Fairview.
Down the Alfie Byrne Road, down past Sheriff Street,
down by the Point and across the toll bridge, down to
Ringsend.
Down through Sandymount, on out past Booterstown, into
Blackrock, down through Monkstown and out into
Dun Laoghaire where we walked out onto the harbour
wall.
I looked into the bag but the fish had died.
And we walked down the harbour in silence.
Sometimes Clare seemed to take my hand like maybe
she wanted to go back.
But I kept going. And she stayed with me.
We'd have to go back soon anyway.
We were running out of land to walk on.
It was just miles and miles of sea.
There was just nowhere left to go anymore.
Except just sort of towards each other for a while.
'What did I say?' My dad said.
'What did I say?'
I was tucking into a bit of Sunday dinner.
'I give it a month! That's what I said. What did I say?'

And to tell you the truth I didn't mind him having
his little moment of triumph.
It was a relief, back home, with my mum and dad and my
sisters.
My room was just as I'd left it, only tidy, and with
clean sheets. And I slept for fifteen hours that night.
And a few nights later Clare called down and we sat in
the kitchen drinking cups of tea, listening to the radio.
She was going mad, she said. Back with the folks.
All evening about how it was doing her head in.
But I knew where it was all going.
She was moving out into another house.
With Declan and some of his mates in their band.
And I was sitting there, telling her that this was
a great idea.
And there was just something stopping us talking about
each other properly. To each other.
Fear? Bewilderment? Disbelief maybe?
That this couldn't be it.
That two people couldn't have found each other this
easily.
We didn't trust it I suppose.
So that was that.
And we soldiered on off down our different roads.
A few weeks later my granny died.
My dad's mum.
And I was sitting there at the funeral, watching my
grandad holding these rosary beads that had belonged
to her, that she'd got from Lourdes.
And I was thinking that maybe there isn't a soul
for every person in the world.
Maybe there's just two.
One for people who go with the flow, and one for all
the people who fight.
Maybe lots of us just share a soul.
So there's no judgement, because there's no point.
It was just this stupid idea.
But it was in my head like a block or something.
Curly haired Patricia was there with me at the funeral.
I'd been getting on the bus a lot recently,

spending a lot of time down there in Parliament Street.

And later on we were in the pub.

And I was staring down at the tiles on the floor.

Because I knew that she was a fighter, and I had the other soul.

And it was more than just a sneaky suspicion that if she was going to fight for me, that I was going to go with the flow.

14
DERMOT

Understandably, I felt like a man who'd been shot up
into the air and all the lads with the nets had fucked
off.
And I was coming down to Earth.
Down to Dublin.
Down the back of the plane in economy.
I was like a zombie.
Standing there outside the airport waiting on a taxi.
And when I got one your man is very much on for a
big chat.
Where had I been? How was it? What did I do for a living
myself?
Holy fuck. I was like one of those figures you see in
the religious paintings where God is pointing for them all
to go to Hell. And they're all looking up at him, very
much feeling the reality of their situation.
I lugged my suitcase into the hall and I could see
Mary and Colm out the back garden.
They'd pulled the kitchen table out on the grass so
they could have their lunch in the sun.
I took a chair and went out and joined them.
We had ham and boiled eggs and brown bread and tea and
a jug of Miwadi orange.
Colm started kicking a ball around but I didn't have
the energy.
I just sat there and told Mary the job was gone.
That it was a mistake.
She laughed at me in a way I understood.
That it was inevitable that things like that should
happen to me. That I was someone to whom things happened.
Colm came over for a drink of orange and absent-mindedly
his arm was on the back of my chair and I could hear
him slurping his drink and he absent-mindedly ran one

of his fingers over the stubble on my cheek.

And that he felt entitled to do that held no humiliation
for me any more, I was too tired, and he was gone anyway.

All the little wars you can fight.

All I had to do to level the playing field was put some
chocolate in front of my wife.

And gradually elevate myself in the world.

And Mary just said to me :

'When I met you, do you know why I chose you?

Because I felt sorry for you.

You looked so wobegon that none of the girls would
dance with you.

You looked so scared there with all the other boys.

And remember. I was no mean looker in them days,
Dermot, I had long legs and I had big boobs and a big
blondy dye job in my hair.

And all the boys you were standing there with, they
couldn't believe me walking past them and asking you
to dance.'

Sure you couldn't believe it yourself!

'What?' You said to me.

You fucking eejit.

What!

I nearly had to drag you to your feet.

You were shaking there on the dancefloor.

You were shaking in my arms.

When I planted a kiss on you, you didn't know what to do.

You got the hang of it.

But it took you a minute.

You held on to me like you were afraid you were going
to wake up and I'd be gone.

I'd been with loads of fellas before you.

But they were all obvious for me.

They all had a smart mouth because their mammies had
turned them into mickey dazzlers telling them the
sun, moon and stars shone out of their heads.

But I shut them up.

Because I wasn't a girl who was afraid to put her hand
down a boy's underpants.

I could make a boy do anything I wanted.

But I chose you, Dermot, because you were alone in the
world.
And I knew you probably would be for the rest of your
life and I decided that I was going to be your friend.
And I know you don't think much of me anymore.
And I don't care you take me for granted and I know
I embarrass you because I never lost all this weight
after Colm.
But I chose you Dermot.
I took you because I knew you'd always need someone to
look after you. And I always will,'
she said.
And it was like I was looking at the three of us there
in the garden from high above.
I could see Colm banging an orange football around
down there against the concrete walls.
And I could see me and Mary sitting there at the table.
Her hand was on the back of my head.
And I was like a hunched figure.
My face falling slowly into her lap.

15
JOE

When you live in close proximity to people in a
home like me, and you're fairly private, you
don't let on if you've got news.
Especially if it's of a highly personal nature.
So to look at me walking around with this photo in
my pocket you wouldn't know a thing.
But Sister Pat clocked me a few times, that I was
miles away.
And I had to get out of her gaze.
Jackie Fennel thought it was bloody Christmas when
I suggested we go and get a bottle of stout at one o'
clock in the afternoon.
And then Mary Larkin got in on the act.
And of course it was a big event now and everyone was
clucking around that the three of us were turning into
alcoholics.
But what can you do?
So there we were hobbling round to Tighe's in the
sunshine.
Jackie was the most agile.
He could still do two things at once.
He was counting out his change, not needing to look
where he was going.
Mary Larkin was going on about what a beautiful
day it was but that didn't stop her ducking into
Tighe's where it was all suitably dark and empty,
and drinking five bottles of Harp.
She was buckled by half two.
We had the place to ourselves.
Jackie kept fiddling with the telly, looking for the
racing, until the barman gave in and let him have the
remote control.
And although I was joining in the general conversation,

I was secretly in a world of my own.
Thinking about Marion Ross and why she'd had this picture
sent to me.
I'd had a look in Jackie's backlog of Independents
and I was right.
She'd passed away a few weeks before.
And I was thinking that she was right in a way.
If I wanted a picture of her, why shouldn't I have it?
And if you can be friends, what are you afraid of?
Except of course what had happened was that I'd fallen
in love with someone I didn't know and that was all there
was about it.
And I never knew her, but when it hits you, it just does.
And maybe if I'd gotten to know her I mightn't even have
liked her, but there you are. I know it exists.
But, I made a decision and your life runs its course.
Maybe I could've battled my way around to us ending
up together.
But what can I say?
It just wasn't in me.
I'm just not made like that.
And a few bottles of stout and two or three balls of
malt later we made our way back around to the home.
Mary Larkin was singing You Are My Sunshine, My Only
Sunshine, but she shut up when Sister Pat hoved into view.
Jackie Fennel was doing a little dance and rubbing
his hands together.
'We're home from the fields!' he says to Sister Pat.
And we sat down and had our dinner.
And of course we were the talk of the bloody town.
'Who's birthday was it?' and all this.
Poor Mary had to hit the sack around seven o'clock.
But Jackie was taking them all on.
He was in great form, slagging them all off.
But then, suddenly, he was fading fast.
And Sister Pat put him to bed.
And I sat there on my own in the dining room.
They didn't think anyone was in there so the
lights were off.
But Sister Pat came and found me and we went down to

her room and had a cup of tea.
And although she was furious I hadn't told her what
I'd gotten in the post, the problem was that she
liked me too much to give me a hard time.
So we just chatted about this and that and she told me
all about where she'd grown up in Roscommon.
And soon enough it was time for bed.
And when I had my pyjamas on I went over to the
table and took these rosary beads out that used to
belong to Liz that she'd gotten in Lourdes.
And I had them sort of wrapped around my fingers.
And naturally I took Marion's photograph out of my
jacket and I looked at it for a little while.
This little girl staring up out at me.
A big smile on her.
Very happy.
Someone I didn't know.
And I was slightly too knackered to finish the
last couple of pages of this cowboy book I was reading.
So I just lay back with Marion's picture in one hand
and Liz's rosary beads in the other.
Thinking about regret and worry.
And when you get to my age, you give up on them because
they don't help anything.
And you generally get tired of regret.
And you're usually just whacked out from worrying.
So I brought these two things together on my chest.
The picture and the beads.
On my heart if you like.
And I did what any Christian would do.
I turned out the light and I went to sleep.